NOR

ENGLAND

1066–1204

Trevor Rowley

C000143420

SHIRE LIVING HISTORIES

How we worked • How we played • How we lived

Published in Great Britain in 2010 by Shire Publications
Ltd, Midland House, West Way, Botley, Oxford OX2 0PH,
United Kingdom.
44-02 23rd Street, Suite 219, Long Island City, NY 11101,
USA.

E-mail: shire@shirebooks.co.uk   www.shirebooks.co.uk

© 2010 Shire Publications.

All rights reserved. Apart from any fair dealing for the
purpose of private study, research, criticism or review, as
permitted under the Copyright, Designs and Patents Act,
1988, no part of this publication may be reproduced,
stored in a retrieval system, or transmitted in any form or
by any means, electronic, electrical, chemical, mechanical,
optical, photocopying, recording or otherwise, without the
prior written permission of the copyright owner.
Enquiries should be addressed to the Publishers.

Every attempt has been made by the Publishers to secure
the appropriate permissions for materials reproduced in
this book. If there has been any oversight we will be happy
to rectify the situation and a written submission should be
made to the Publishers.

A CIP catalogue record for this book is available from the
British Library.

Shire Living Histories no. 8.   ISBN-13: 978 0 74780 800 8

Trevor Rowley has asserted his right under the Copyright,
Designs and Patents Act, 1988, to be identified as the
author of this book.

Designed by Myriam Bell Design, France and typeset in
Perpetua, Jenson Text and Gill Sans.

Printed in China through Worldprint Ltd.

10 11 12 13 14   10 9 8 7 6 5 4 3 2 1

DEDICATION

For Jane and Norman, a Venetian lion.

ACKNOWLEDGEMENTS

Aerofilm, page 8; Mick Aston, page 14; Ashmolean
Museum, page 71; T. W. Ball, pages 19 (bottom), 20–1;
The citizens and town of Bayeux, pages 9 (left and right),
16 (bottom), 40 (bottom), 49 (bottom), 55 (bottom);
Bodleian Library, pages 22, 24, 27, 28–29, 32 (bottom),
33 (top), 41, 42 (top), 43, 46, 52, 54 (top and bottom),
55 (top), 62 (top and bottom), 63 (top), 64 (top), 65 (top
and bottom), 66, 70 (top and bottom), 72, 74, 75
(bottom); British Library, pages 6, 11, 34 (top and
bottom), 50, 60; British Museum, pages 49 (top), 63
(bottom); Cambridge Aerial Photographs, pages 18, 48; H.
Clarke, page 42 (bottom); English Heritage, pages 4, 19
(top), 30, 37, 38; W. H. Godfrey, page 75 (top); Brian Paul
Hindle, page 56; Susan James, page 76; Museum of
London, page 64 (bottom); The National Archives, page
10; Nicholas Orme, page 69; C. Platt, page 77 (bottom);
Derek Renn, page 13; Alan Sorrell, page 17 (bottom); York
Museums 51 (top). Original artwork on pages 44–5 by
Graham Turner, © Shire Publications. All other images are
from the author's collection.

COVER IMAGE
A scene of an Anglo-Norman baronial hall (see pages
43–5).

Shire Publications is supporting the Woodland Trust, the UK's leading woodland conservation charity, by funding the dedication of trees.

CONTENTS

PREFACE

THE YEAR 1066 is the date in English history that virtually everyone knows – and most people recognise that the arrival of the Normans and demise of Anglo-Saxon England brought deep changes to the way of life of the entire country. The physical manifestations, massive castles on great mounds and solid churches with round arches, are just the very visible tip of an iceberg that included military and technological changes – knights fighting on horseback – political changes – a new ruling class that owed everything to the king – and even linguistic changes – French was used alongside English for a century, and has left many traces in our speech today.

Domesday Book, compiled just twenty years after the conquest, reveals the thoroughgoing nature of the revolution that William the Conqueror wrought, when the proud tradition of the Anglo-Saxon freeman was overtaken by the Norman institution of the much less independent villeins working with the manorial system. Throughout the following century and a half, energetic monarchs ruling an unusually centralised country meant that these changes became consolidated and ingrained in the nation's way of life – to such an extent that many people think of 1066 as the beginning of English history itself.

Yet, as with all revolutions, some things stayed the same, and many aspects of everyday life – the rhythms of the farming year, food and drink, birth and death – saw little change with the arrival of the Normans. In this book Trevor Rowley offers an authoritative and wide-ranging look at all this, offering a coherent survey of life in the century and a half that followed the arrival of the Normans.

Peter Furtado
General editor

Opposite: Orford Castle, Suffolk, was built by Henry II who made it his East Anglian seat. It cost £1,413 9s 2d. The circular keep here was the first royal departure from the traditional rectangular ground plan. The larger-than-usual windows show that comfort was a serious consideration here.

triumphator magnificus potent adquisita subiugau
de bello ubi tumpharat fundau. Regnau añis xvi. z aplui

trem eí receperit z ipm cauert mscripsit fatigauit
Aula Westm onstruit. tandem sagra piit psm rer

õ rer
prii põ
onem eí

 nicus se
ger rã
xxx̄ vii

nicus̄ uir potens z sapiens iurau leges sci eduardi iñ
s tene. sz psm uicat frem suũ noluit. Hobsie cenobiũ de
o ubi sepult iac; fundau z reparu onstruit karl. Regnau añ
xxxviii z circiter dimidiũ.

Iste Stephanus miles strenuissim onibz;
dubus casibz; belloz interfuit. Iste abbaciam de
fundauit. In qua ipe z Eustach filius eí z ẽ
uxor eí iacent sepulti. Iste Regnauit añis. x

THE NORMAN CONQUEST

O N SATURDAY 16 OCTOBER 1066, Duke William II of Normandy defeated an Anglo-Saxon army led by King Harold at the Battle of Hastings. The *Anglo-Saxon Chronicle* recorded that 'King Harold was killed ... and the French remained masters of the field'. On Christmas Day the same year William was crowned King of England in Westminster Abbey, initiating the Norman dynasty of English monarchs. These momentous events would have had little immediate impact on those Anglo-Saxons who had not been involved at Hastings or were not affected by William's marauding armies, which had taken uneasy control of south-east England.

Initially, William intended to rule the kingdom in the same manner that Scandinavian monarchs such as Canute had done earlier in the century. He would have preserved Anglo-Saxon governmental and church infrastructures, and many English landowners would have maintained their estates. If these were indeed his intentions, rebellions in various parts of England caused him to change his mind radically. Early in 1068, King Harold's mother, Gytha, led an uprising in the south-west; the subsequent siege of Exeter and its aftermath marked the turning point in relations between the English and their conquerors. Thereafter, the policy of co-existence turned into one of determined domination.

William's real problems were in the north, where the appointment of Robert of Commines as earl of Northumbria was deeply unpopular. He was described as 'one of those persons who paid the wages of their followers by licensing their ravages and murders'. Following an uprising in Durham in late 1069, William determined on crushing the English rebellion and marched north. The subsequent notorious campaign became known as the 'Harrying of the North', when it was claimed that the city of York 'and the whole district round it was destroyed by the French with the sword, famine and flames'. Simeon of Durham recalled the putrefying corpses which littered the highways

Opposite:
The four Norman kings holding cathedrals, from a thirteenth-century manuscript. Top: William I and William II; bottom: Henry I and Stephen. From *The Historia Anglorum* by Mathew Paris, 1259, St Albans.

and the pestilence which followed the massacres. It was reported that so many died that there was nobody left to bury them. No village was inhabited between York and Durham, and the land remained uncultivated for nine years.

There were other rebellions during the remainder of William's reign, including that of the shadowy figure of Hereward in East Anglia, but after the harrying of the north there was no chance that the Normans would be displaced.

Aerial view of Durham, naturally defended by a loop of the River Wear, with the castle guarding the narrowest point. The city was at the heart of the uprising against William that prompted the 'Harrying of the North'. The great Norman cathedral is in the centre of the picture.

By the time the Domesday Book, William's inventory of his new kingdom, was completed in 1086 the Anglo-Saxon aristocracy and Church leaders had been replaced by Normans and their allies. There had also been an almost complete transfer of land from Saxon thegns to continental lords. The Domesday Book provides a sobering record of these changes – out of the 13,000 holdings which appear in the great survey, only a handful remained under Saxon control. The order and detail of the Domesday Book suggests a calm transfer of land from Saxon to Norman, but the situation on the ground must have been very different, with much local violence, injustice and confusion. Under the new Norman regime, bishops and abbots held twenty-six per cent of the land and the remainder was in the hands of 190 earls and barons. A dozen leading members of the new aristocracy controlled a quarter of England.

Although there were far fewer Normans in England than Anglo-Saxons, the impact of the Conquest was eventually felt at every level, most notably in the rigid restructuring of society that is conventionally known as the 'Feudal System'. The king was at the top of a social pyramid, and land was handed down through a series of layers of tenants in return for a range of services.

Above left: King Harold, on the left, is killed at the Battle of Hastings on the Bayeux Tapestry. The picture of him with an arrow in his eye is the only evidence there is that he died in this way.

Above: Scene from the Bayeux Tapestry showing Normans torching a Saxon house before the Battle of Hastings. An escaping mother is remonstrating with the soldiers.

Extract from the
Domesday Book
showing the
entires for land
held by the
archbishop of
Canterbury and
bishops in
Oxfordshire.

Continental landholders, be they bishops, earls or knights, became
the new Anglo-Norman 'lords'.

Under the feudal system, below the king were the earls and
counts. These were honorific titles, given to a few men holding great
estates, and in 1200 there were just sixteen earldoms in England. The
term 'baron' was used to describe the greater tenants-in-chief of the
Crown, although there was no clear definition of what constituted a

barony until Magna Carta (1215). Generally, they were powerful secular lords with a household of five or more knights, with an annual income of about £200.

The term 'knight' had several meanings. They were cavalrymen, as depicted on the Bayeux Tapestry, but they were also landholders, lower than the barons and higher than freemen. In the Angevin period (post 1154), when there were between four thousand five hundred and five thousand knights, it was decreed that only knights could serve on certain juries. A knight imprisoned for debt could lose his land, but his horse was immune 'lest he who has been raised to the dignity of knight be forced to go on foot'. The king increasingly accepted a payment in lieu of military service. This was known as *scutage* or shield money, with which the Crown hired mercenaries in France, where most fighting took place. Thus knights were no longer required to be resident in the baronial and were granted manors in place of their maintenance. By 1200 the knight had replaced the Anglo-Saxon thegn as the backbone of local landownership.

A crusader knight in military dress, with helm, lance and pennon. Westminster Psalter, c. 1250.

Manors were the Norman unit of rural organisation. In its simplest form a manor consisted of one village with a single lord. The lord with his free and unfree tenants cultivated the village lands communally. The lord reserved for his own use a portion of the estate known as the *demesne* or home farm, which was cultivated for him by his villeins in return for their holdings.

'Freemen', who constituted twelve per cent of the population in 1086, held up to a hundred acres. The freemen paid money rents and performed only relatively light and occasional work for the lord. During the twelfth century their numbers decreased, as many of them joined the ranks of villeins in response to a tightening of the feudal system.

Below the freemen were 'villeins', who in 1086 accounted for forty per cent of the rural population. Villeins owed two or three days' work a week to the lord, with additional days during busy seasons of the farming year. They had a few oxen of their own and holdings of fifteen or thirty acres. 'Bordars' and 'cottars' held between three and five acres and accounted for thirty per cent of the rural population in 1086.

In 1086 specialised workers such as millers, blacksmiths, wheelwrights and swineherds appeared as villeins, bordars or cottars. At the bottom were the serfs or slaves, who constituted ten per cent of the population. Slaves had no property rights and could be bought and sold by the lord. Serfs largely disappeared during the twelfth century, as they were absorbed into the ranks of the unfree peasants.

The Domesday Book only recorded heads of household and did not cover monks, nuns or those living in castles. Nevertheless, the population of England at this time has been tentatively estimated at between two and three million people. There were 112 boroughs in 1086, the largest of which were Norwich, York and Lincoln, which had populations of between four and five thousand people. England's two capital cities, London and Winchester, were omitted from the Domesday Book. Winchester was surveyed in the mid-twelfth century, but if London ever had a similar survey it has since disappeared. During the twelfth century the population grew and this was reflected in the number of new towns, many of which were

Twelfth-century blind arcading on the west front of the church at the Cistercian abbey of Castle Acre, Norfolk.

speculative attempts to attract and monopolise trade by a king, bishop or knight. It was also a period of agricultural expansion, and throughout England the process known as 'assarting' brought areas of former fenland, heathland and woodland into cultivation.

On the Bayeux Tapestry William is shown holding the papal banner at critical moments during the Conquest; and papal support helped persuade the Church and most English people to accept William as their new king. William's half-brother Odo was bishop of Bayeux and played a significant role in the planning and execution of the Conquest. He was made earl of Kent and rewarded with extensive landholdings, and in 1086 was the third-wealthiest man in England. William also relied heavily on churchmen to act as his administrators.

The distribution of motte and bailey castles in Great Britain and Ireland. The concentration of castles in the Welsh Marches reflects the unsettled nature of the region in the post-Conquest period as well as their use in the early stages of the conquest of Wales.

The church, many examples of which remain today as monuments to Norman communities, was the nucleus of village activity. The villagers gathered here not only for religious observances on Sundays and Holy Days but also for festivities, dancing and sometimes to trade. Parish priests were mainly of humble birth and in addition to caring for the souls of the community would have had to work their own church land (glebe), which lay in strips intermingled with those of their parishioners. All manorial landholders were liable to a tithe of one-tenth of agricultural produce to support their church. The Council of Westminster (1175) listed 'grain, wine, fruit, new-born livestock, wool, cheese, flax and hemp' as taxable.

The years following the Conquest witnessed an increase in the founding of new monasteries. The Cluniacs were the first, founding priories at Lewes in 1077 and Castle Acre (Norfolk). The Cistercian order had the greatest influence, spreading widely across England and Wales, often in remote areas such as the Yorkshire moors. The Cistercians often drew on local people to work the land needed to establish new abbeys and in this way opened up the Church to people usually excluded from religious life.

THE IMPACT OF THE NORMANS ON ANGLO-SAXON LIFE

MANY OF THE NORMANS who took over England became extremely prosperous on the basis of the lands they acquired after the Conquest. Initially some of this wealth returned to Normandy to build abbeys and churches, but increasingly it went into creating a new colonial architecture in England. Above all it was the castle which defined the Norman Conquest. Orderic Vitalis (1075–*c*. 1142) observed:

> The King rode into all the remote parts of his kingdom and fortified strategic sites against enemy attack. For the fortifications called castles by the Normans were scarcely known in the English provinces so the English in spite of their courage and love of fighting could put up only a weak resistance to their enemies.

Castles were built by all landholders, from the king down to the small Welsh Marcher knight. In addition to establishing a power base, the castle provided living accommodation for the lord, his household and his knights. William built castles in county towns, creating combined military and administrative strongholds, and by 1086 there were at least fifty in England. The Domesday Book records that there was considerable destruction to accommodate castles and to create a clear line of fire around them. At Norwich, for instance, where a motte with two baileys was inserted into the central part of the town, ninety-eight houses and two churches were destroyed; at Lincoln one hundred and sixty houses were destroyed, and at Shrewsbury fifty-one. At Oxford the Domesday Book records that only 243 houses were capable of paying geld; the remaining 478 were 'so devastated and destroyed that they could not render any tax'.

The most common form of castle introduced by the Normans was the earth-and-timber 'motte and bailey'. The term derives from the

Opposite: Aerial view of Old Sarum. The ringwork in the centre of an Iron Age hill fort housed the Bishop of Salisbury's castle. In the foreground are the footings of the first cathedral at Salisbury, dating from 1092.

Norman French '*motte*', meaning mound, and 'bailey', the surrounding enclosure. An early twelfth-century account from Flanders explains:

> It is the custom of the nobles of that region ... in order to defend themselves from their enemies to make a hill of earth, as high as they can, and encircle it with a ditch as broad and deep as possible. They surround the upper edge of this hill with a very strong wall of hewn logs, placing towers on the circuit, according to their means. Inside this wall they plant their house [domus], or keep [arcem], which overlooks the whole thing. The entrance of this fortress is only by a bridge, which rises from the counterscarp of the ditch...

The royal castle keep at Norwich, built c. 1130. This was a palatial hall keep partly constructed with Caen stone from Normandy. The castle was substantially restored to the original design in the nineteenth century.

The motte and bailey castle was easily built, using enforced Saxon labour, and if destroyed could be rebuilt quickly. Hundreds of these castles were built, with the greatest concentration in the Welsh Marches, but by 1200 most earth-and-timber castles had been abandoned or transformed. If they were not rebuilt in stone they tended to be replaced by more comfortable manor houses.

William overseeing the building of a motte and bailey castle at Hastings. He is holding the Papal banner, which he carried throughout the campaign against King Harold and the Anglo-Saxons.

The castle motte at Oxford, built by Robert D'Oilly in the 1070s. Its construction involved the destruction of many town houses.

The most impressive Norman buildings were the great stone castle keeps (French *donjon*). The keep was used for storing produce, armaments and equipment and also providing a hall and living space. In addition to being more durable and less vulnerable to fire, keeps were used to impress Norman power and prestige upon the conquered English. Indeed, the Norman lords did not need their new stone castles to fight off rebellions by the English as much as they needed them in wars between each other.

The civil war between Stephen and Matilda (1135–54), known as the Anarchy, saw the construction of dozens of unlawful fortifications. By 1154 it is estimated that there were some 274 active castles, of which only forty-nine were in the hands of King Stephen.

A reconstruction of the motte and bailey castle with its shell keep at Totnes, Devon.

The great hall keep at Castle Rising, Norfolk, contained within a large ringwork. It was built by William de Albini II in the mid-twelfth century. Albini married Henry I's widow and was said to be 'intolerably puffed up'. The exterior is richly decorated in the Norfolk tradition.

There were extensive siegeworks, and even some churches and monasteries were fortified. Monks were ejected from the abbeys at Bridlington, Coventry and Ramsey, while ringworks were erected round churches at Merrington (Durham) and St Martin, Thetford (Norfolk). The aftermath of the Anarchy saw a significant tightening of royal control under Henry II and John, both of whom reduced the number of baronial castles and almost doubled the number of royal fortifications.

The crusades in the twelfth century resulted in new forms of castle being built, incorporating ideas of fortification brought in from the Middle East. The most notable feature of such castles was the introduction of the round tower. Polygonal and circular keeps as well as shell keeps on the tops of mottes began to feature in later castles, although they were never particularly popular in England.

The great age of castle building in England was over by the end of King John's reign in 1216. The idea of combining the main accommodation in one defensible structure, keep or motte and bailey, served the Normans well, but created uncomfortable living

The Bishop of Winchester's Wolvesey Palace at Winchester. It was built by the prince-bishop Henry de Blois, King Stephen's brother.

conditions. Consequently many smaller castles were left to decay as military strategies changed, and although some royal and baronial castles like Windsor had their accommodation updated regularly, others became prisons or arsenals, and eventually quarries.

Reconstruction of Wolvesey Palace, Winchester, c. 1200. In two of the courtyards there was a *lavatorium* with running water.

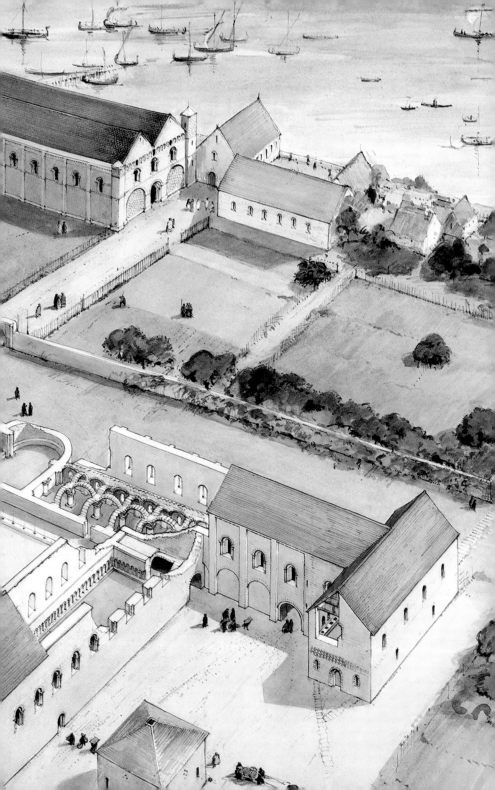

Previous spread: Reconstruction of the abbey and royal palace at Westminster, c. AD 1100. The abbey church, which was based on the design of Jumieges in Normandy, was consecrated on Christmas Day 1065 and was at the heart of the momentous events of the following year. The Great Hall was completed under William II.

Hunter spearing an antelope in woodland, from a Peterborough bestiary, c. 1200. (MS. Ashmole 1511, 14r)

Castles belonging to high-status individuals were required to perform other functions such as the provision of an administrative and judicial centre. The Tower of London served the dual function of providing a military base and palatial accommodation for the king and his family. The royal suite included a hall, a chamber, garderobes and a chapel. Not all royal palaces were fortified, and the palace at Westminster was only defended with a perimeter wall. Royal palaces such as Windsor and Woodstock were located close to royal forests and served as bases for the itinerant royal court and council.

The palaces of the Norman prince-bishops were as imposing as those of their lay contemporaries. This reflected their central and sometimes decisive political role in twelfth-century England. The Norman bishops of Winchester built a great palatial complex at Wolvesey, which contained 'a true hall, a place of gathering, not merely for feeding and sleeping large numbers of retainers, but for meeting and ceremonial'. At Old Sarum (Salisbury) there was a bishop's palace inside a castle, both placed within a prehistoric hill fort, the ruins of which form one of the most dramatic monuments in England. Bishop Roger of Caen built a complex here that included two halls, one for his palace and one for the castle.

The Normans introduced forest law – important new legislation covering the right to keep and hunt deer, to appoint forest officials, to hold forest courts and to levy fines. Royal forests not only provided hunting for the king and his supporters, they also ensured a supply of game for the court table. Poachers were punished with a severity – death or mutilation – not known under common law. At one stage in the twelfth century up to a third of England was royal forest, and forest law became increasingly restrictive.

The creation of a forest made a deep impression upon the minds of contemporaries. John of Worcester alleged that in creating the New Forest William I had depopulated a fruitful and prosperous countryside and destroyed

houses and churches to make way for the deer. Popular belief declared that the death of William Rufus while he was hunting in the New Forest was an act of divine retribution for the impious act of his father.

Medieval parks differed from forests in that they were defined by a boundary consisting of a ditch and wooden pale or in certain areas a stone wall. Deer leaps, which allowed animals into the park but not out, were built around the perimeter. The parks were for the retention of deer, at first roe and red deer, but later exclusively fallow deer. At Devizes, Bishop Roger of Salisbury created a park adjacent to his new castle and castle town and created a classic example of Norman seigneurial landscape design, as the large oval-shaped park to the west mirrors exactly the shape of the town and castle to the east.

Relatively few new place-names were introduced by the Normans. The exceptions were where a completely new settlement was laid out; for example, the place-name Sheene was replaced by Richmond (strong hill), Biscopestone by Montacute (pointed hill) and Tattershall by Pontefract (broken bridge). The majority contain the adjective *beau* or *bel*, in names like Beaulieu (beautiful place), Beaumont (beautiful hill) or Beaudesert (beautiful wilderness). Such names were normally applied to new communities, abbeys or castles. Some places were given names incorporating the element *mal* (poor or bad). Macegarth (Yorkshire) was from Melasart (bad clearing), and Malpas (Cheshire) refers to marshy ground. Haltemprice (Yorkshire), a priory of Augustinian canons, comes from the French *haut emprise* (great undertaking), and Dieulacres (Staffordshire) means 'may God increase it'. Boulge (Suffolk) means 'uncultivated land covered with heather'; Bruern (Oxfordshire) refers to 'heath'; and Kearsney (Kent) 'the place where cress grows'.

Norman personal names were sometimes attached to an earlier Anglo-Saxon place-name. The largest group was compounded with Old English *tun* (farmstead or village), as in Williamston (Northumberland) from William, Howton (Herefordshire) from Hugh, Rowlstone (Herefordshire) from Rolf, and Walterstone (Herefordshire) from Walter. There are also many village names where a French family name has been attached to an Old English name. This was done in order to distinguish manors with similar names for taxation purposes; for example, Stoke Mandeville, Bury Pomery, Ashby-de-la-Zouch, Croome d'Abitot and Shepton Mallet. Occasionally the names have coalesced as in the case of Stokesay (Shropshire), from Stoke-de-Say.

noctibz.

oyser
cū dñi
locu
in monte sig
scm petrū q̄
dño locutus
de profundit
suoꝝ secretoꝝ

oram
facie
moyſi
morte cū di
dixerūt filii
ad aaron. Fā
nob̄ deos q̄ n̄
precedant· q̄
ſi enī huic n̄
mus q̄ō accit
et dyrit illis
ton. Tollire in
res aureaſ· q̄
cum ille acce
ſet· fecit eis
tulū q̄flatil

FAMILY LIFE

IRRESPECTIVE OF SOCIAL CLASS, childbirth was dangerous and a healthy child was seen as a gift from heaven. When a mother went into labour she was attended by a midwife, but in the event of complications there was little to be done. Up to five per cent of infants died during childbirth. Death from disease and accident during infancy remained high and the mortality rate for children up to the age of five was as high as thirty per cent. The umbilical cord would be burnt on the family hearth after birth. Water would have been available when a woman gave birth, not only for medicinal purposes, but for the baby to be baptised if he or she was about to die as it was believed that infants did not have a soul until baptised. Chapels in remote areas were used for infant baptism, although rights to the sacraments of marriage and burial were withheld by the mother parish church.

Most babies in Norman England would have been taken to church on the day they were born by the father, godparents and midwife – the mother was not allowed to attend church for several weeks after giving birth. The priest met the party at the church door and put salt in the baby's mouth to represent the reception of wisdom and to exorcise demons. Abandoned babies were often found with untied umbilical cords or salt nearby to indicate that they had not been baptised. The priest would anoint the child, who would then be immersed in the font and named. The christening gown was an important garment, made of white linen and perhaps decorated with seed pearls in wealthier families. During the first year some children, particularly those in noble households, were swaddled and wet-nurses were employed.

Children were considered to be adult at twelve, the age at which it was acceptable for girls to marry, although betrothal at as young an age as seven was common. Peasant children would have helped with housework and on the land from an early age. They would have had no formal education and would have expected to follow their parents' life and work pattern. The children of priests, knights and the

Opposite:
Infant baptism depicted on an early-thirteenth-century manuscript. (MS. Bodl. 270b, 54r)

Heath Chapel, Shropshire. Such chapelries had the right to baptise infants because the mother church (Stoke St Milborough) was too far away if a child was in danger of dying.

aristocracy normally had some tuition in grammar. A range of toys made of leather, wood, clay and metal, mainly from baronial or urban households, have been found; these include rattles, dolls, spinning tops and miniature boats and carts. Gerald of Wales (1147–1223), the cleric and chronicler of his times, relates how as a small boy he built churches out of sand while his elder brothers preferred the more traditional sand castles. The twelfth-century writer Alexander Nequam (1157–1217) described an upper-class chamber, where a group of young girls were sewing and embroidering with leather thimbles on their thumbs and the tips of the fingers of their gloves open, so that they could do delicate work.

Freemen came of age at fifteen, but burgesses 'when they can count money and measure cloth'. Training to be a knight began at seven, when as an apprentice (squire) he would serve in another lord's baronial household. At twenty-one the squire would undergo a dubbing ceremony, which initially was in the form of a blow to the neck, followed by an admonition to conduct himself with courage and loyalty.

The Church defined a legal marriage as an agreement between two parties; an exchange of words between man and woman (the troth-plight) was all that was needed. Vows would be given in the church porch or other public place and would have been binding. Marriage contracts were often verbal, but they involved a payment or *merchet* to the lord. At this stage there was no formalised marriage vow and a Canterbury witness (*c.* 1200) claimed that he was unsure which words he had used to contract his wife only a year before. When a marriage had been agreed upon it was sealed with a betrothal ceremony held before witnesses. The nobility often arranged such ceremonies after a child was seven, although the wedding had to wait until the bride was twelve and the bridegroom fourteen. After the betrothal the banns would be read out on three occasions, but not during Advent or Lent. On the day of the wedding the bride and groom would meet at the church door; here the groom announced the dower his wife would receive and gave her gold or silver as a symbol of the dower and a ring. The couple would then enter the church and kneel under a pall for a blessing. If they had borne children together before the marriage, they too would kneel under the pall and the blessing was deemed to make them legitimate.

Weddings were an excuse for a communal celebration and Bishop Poore (*c.* 1231) ordered that marriages should 'be celebrated reverently and with honour, not with laughter or sport, or in taverns'. Ales known as 'bride ales' were brewed for the occasion, the profits of which went to the new bride. In some instances the priest would also bless the bridal bedchamber and bed.

Intermarriage between Normans and Anglo-Saxon families became common and *c.* 1180 Richard fitz Neal wrote that:

Infant Christ in swaddling clothes. (MS. Bodl. 270b, 37v)

> nowadays, when English and Normans live close together and marry and give in marriage to each other, the nations are so mixed that it can scarcely be decided (I mean in the case of freemen) who is of English birth and who of Norman.

Most marriages involved a contract covering property and goods. If there was no dower involved, then marriage was often not thought necessary at all. A prevailing view in the early twelfth century was that a marriage was not fully legal until it was consummated, and formal marriage was sometimes delayed until the woman became pregnant. Wealthy widows and heiresses were vulnerable and some were sold in marriage to the highest bidder or to the king's friends. In order 'to remain a widow as long as she pleases' or 'to marry herself to whom she pleases', ladies were forced to pay a substantial fine. This practice was particularly prevalent in the reigns of Richard I and John, who were raising money for overseas wars. The story of Christina of Markyate's long resistance to her parents' marriage plans is well known. It is in the form of a tract commending Christina's piety, steadfastness and eventual success in taking up her chosen life as a religious solitary. The background story of parental coercion must have been all too common.

Sometimes extreme methods of persuasion were used; for instance, Oliver the Angevin was imprisoned and held in fetters until he agreed to marry a certain woman. There is no evidence to support the popular myth that in the early Middle Ages the lord had the right to claim the virginity of a new estate bride on the wedding night, the so-called *droit de seigneur*. However, a lord was entitled to *leirwite*

At left, a wedding procession is accompanied by musicians while on the right the bride and groom meet the priest outside the church. From a Flemish version of *The Romance of Alexander*. (MS. Bodl. 264, pt. 1, 105r)

(literally, a fine for lying down) from women who were not married but were sexually active. Likewise, *childwite* was a fine levied for giving birth out of wedlock.

From the middle of the eleventh century the Church tried to stop priests marrying. The Council of Winchester (1076) decreed that no canon should marry, but that priests who lived in the countryside and were already married did not have to send their wives away. Unmarried priests were to remain celibate, and bishops were not to ordain priests unless they gave a vow that they were not married.

The Church also banned marriage between people who were closely related (consanguinity). It was forbidden to marry a relative or one's dead wife's relative 'to the seventh degree'. This could constitute a severe restriction to the choice of marriage partner in the countryside, within what were relatively closed communities.

We see something of the male attitude to women and marriage in this advice to the 'courteous man':

> If for a wife you are looking, be on your guard lest you marry
> Daughters or widows of these, else all your plans will miscarry:
> Celibate priests and canons, torturers, beadles malicious,
> Actors, or those who lend money; any such woman is vicious.
> Never speak lewdly concerning those of the feminine gender;
> … Always be properly grateful; cherish, revere, and adore her.
>
> (*Facetos*)

At this time there was no recognised divorce from a valid marriage, which could only be broken by legal separation or by nullification.

The commonest cause was consanguinity, which was used by the aristocracy as a means of obtaining divorce on demand and holding on to dowry estates. Maud de Laigle was married to Robert, earl of Northumberland shortly before he rebelled against William II in 1095. Eventually a divorce was arranged and *c.* 1107 she married Nigel d'Aubigny, one of Henry I's chief supporters. Unable to bear him a child, she herself was divorced on the grounds that 'she had been the wife of one of his relatives', and in the process she lost the Mowbray estates. Similarly, King John divorced his first wife on grounds of consanguinity, but nevertheless held on to the extensive Gloucester estates that had formed part of her dower.

There was a significant change in the choice of personal names after the Conquest as traditional Saxon names became unfashionable. When he arrived in Normandy in 1085, Orderic Vitalis recalled that 'the name Vitalis was given me in place of my English name, which sounded harsh to the Normans'. Another young boy was given the Saxon name Tostig, but 'when his youthful companions mocked the name' he changed it to William.

This process of cultural imitation led to the wholesale adoption of Norman names by the native population. Within a century of the Conquest, three-quarters of the burgesses of Canterbury had continental names. William, Robert, Richard, Roger and Hugh had become the most common names at all levels of society. Surnames were unusual before the fourteenth century. It was, however, customary to have a byname or nickname. Roger Deus salvet dominus, 'God-save-the-ladies', was one of the more unusual given to a twelfth-century Essex landholder.

Home and Neighbourhood

THE OVERWHELMING MAJORITY OF THE POPULATION of Norman England lived in the countryside and were tied to the land they farmed. It has been estimated that in 1086 thirty-five per cent of land was arable, twenty-five per cent meadow or pasture, fifteen per cent woodland and the remaining twenty-five per cent commonland or waste.

In 1086 many villages were still little more than scattered hamlets, not yet settled into the nucleated pattern of the medieval village. However, some settlements like Isham (Northamptonshire) had been replanned by the lord and peasants, with a green and a church in the centre, surrounded by peasant houses, with arable land combined into two or three large open fields. By 1200 this pattern was typical of much of England.

Village houses were almost all built of wood, wattle and mud and were single storey. The roof was thatched with straw or reeds or later with wooden tiles. The house was known as a toft and the land around was a croft, which was enclosed by ditches or hedges and used as a garden, with outbuildings. From about 1180 there was a significant change with the adoption of stone foundations or sills in parts of the country where stone was readily available. This helped prolong the life of the superstructure by raising it above the damp ground.

At Goltho (Lincolnshire), an excavated eleventh-century house measured 9 feet by 24 feet and was divided between a living area with a central hearth and a byre. This was a longhouse, where animals lived seasonally under the same roof as the family, providing much-needed warmth in winter. The windows would have been unglazed, but would have had shutters. A family, with perhaps four children at home, would all live in the single room, and cook over the open hearth. The floors consisted of packed clay and were regularly swept. Peasant inventories for Norman England indicate that they had few possessions. There was only space for a few furnishings, such as a table, stools and possibly a chest.

Opposite:
A reconstruction of the deserted medieval village of Wharram Percy, Yorkshire, showing the manor houses and villeins' houses surrounded by their open field strips.

The excavated footings of a stone-based peasants' house at Upton in the Gloucestershire Cotswolds. The gaps for the two opposite doorways are at the top of the photograph and the hearth next to the top marker pole.

Sacks of straw covered with coarse blankets or sheepskins would have served as beds. Wealthier peasants might own a bedstand. The peasant household would have contained utensils made of straw, wood and ceramic; only the wealthier would have owned iron pots. Ceramic pots made locally would have been used for storage and cooking. A survey of the possessions of a widow called Goda on her death, at Alton (Hampshire), recorded that she had a house with a chamber, two pigs, one cow, one leaden vessel and sundry utensils. This was very unusual for a twelfth-century peasant.

Only the elite – the lord, the priest and the reeve (the lord's steward) – and some of the wealthier peasants enjoyed more substantial houses and living conditions. Excavations of manor houses and even churches show that they were sometimes built on the sites of earlier peasant houses, indicating that such dwellings were expendable. Most twelfth-century manor houses would have been constructed of wood and consisted of the hall, the chamber and kitchen. The hall was the focus for the lord and his family, who ate there with their servants. The chamber was for the privacy of the lord and his wife. In Henry II's reign, Roald of Chelsfield leased the manor of Lenborough (Bucks) from Reading Abbey for £3 a year. It consisted of a hall, a chamber, a kitchen, two barns, a sheepfold and a cow byre. The demesne land included 12 acres of winter ploughing and 18 acres of spring ploughing. A number of stone manor houses were built in the later twelfth century for wealthier lords, providing a more spacious and comfortable living environment.

The arable land of the village was divided into two or three open fields, on which a scheme of crop rotation would be

Flemish thirteenth-century calendar, January. A man in a cloak warms his feet before a fire. He is drinking from a bowl with a laid table behind him. Birds and cured meat hangs from a pole above. (MS. Add. A. 46, 1r)

A woman milking a cow, from a thirteenth-century English bestiary. (MS. Bodl. 764, 41v)

Norman manor house at Boothby Pagnell, Lincolnshire. The hall and separate lord's sleeping quarters are on the first floor and reached by an external staircase. There is a large hooded fireplace in the hall. Fireplaces were being introduced into lords' houses in the later twelfth century.

operated. One field would be given over to winter-sown crops, a second to spring-sown crops, and the third left uncultivated to allow it to recover fertility in time for the next year's sowing. Each of the fields would be divided into furlongs and each of the furlongs into strips known as 'selions'. Within each field some of the strips would be held by the tenants of the village, some by the rector, and some held 'in demesne' by the manorial lord. Schemes of crop rotation could become complex, providing wheat for sale at market, barley

A wheeled plough with oxen, from a copy of Augustine's *City of God*, produced in Canterbury in the early twelfth century. The Domesday Book listed 80,000 plough-teams working in England in 1086.

Peasants harvesting, from an eleventh-century calendar.

for brewing and oats for fodder. The system of co-operative agriculture was also applied to pasture and meadowland, which was divided up between the community.

Village life revolved around the agricultural calendar. In spring the animals grazed in the pasture and seed was sown. Summer was the busiest time, particularly when the harvests of wheat, barley, rye, hay, vegetables and fruit were being gathered. In autumn the animals grazed on the remains of the crops, providing manure for the fields, which were then ploughed.

On most manors there was an area of commonland where landholders could graze a specified number of animals. They would also have rights to browse pigs and collect fallen branches, for fuel and building, in the manorial woods. For a villein with a small holding the commons provided a lifeline, for he might keep cattle, geese or even beehives there to make honey.

The manor court was held every three weeks and presided over by the lord or his reeve. It dealt with quarrels and infringements relating to the running of the manorial estate, such as overgrazing on the commons, illicitly diverting the millstream or encroaching onto a neighbour's strip in the open fields. Incidents involving violence and theft were also dealt with locally. The court could also deal with such wide-ranging offences as infringements of the highway, the receiving and harbouring of strangers, the use of false weights and measures, the frequenting of taverns by night and the clipping of coins. Murder and more serious crimes would have been tried by the king's itinerant courts. Some disputes were solved by the traditional Norman remedy of trial by combat.

Apart from the manor, the parish church would have been the main focus of community life. The lord prayed in the chancel, while the rest of the villagers used the nave. The parish priest was appointed by the lord of the manor, who would provide him with a dwelling. New parish churches were constructed in the Norman style. This evolved from an austere neoclassical to a highly ornamented style during the course of the twelfth century.

In 1066 towns were already a recognisable feature in England. In Norman England these grew in importance as military, religious and administrative centres. In the one hundred and fifty years after Domesday the number of towns in England more than doubled. Some towns developed around a new monastery. At Bury St Edmunds King Canute had founded a new abbey in the first half of the eleventh century and during the twenty years between 1066 and the making of Domesday more than three hundred houses were built on land that had previously been used for agriculture. The two largest towns in England were London, with at least ten thousand inhabitants, and Winchester, with around six thousand. Other large towns at the time

A remarkable late Norman carving at Kilpeck, Herefordshire. Tympanum with tree of life surrounded by voussoirs with grotesques, beakheads and signs of the zodiac.

The heavily restored Norman gate-tower to the monastery at Bury St Edmunds.

included Norwich, York and Lincoln, with populations of between four and five thousand each.

Increasingly, trade was the focus of the boroughs. Many served their local areas with goods like livestock, fish and salt. A settlement had developed around salt mining at Droitwich in Worcestershire. Domesday records thirteen salt houses in Droitwich, from which three salt workers paid 300 measures of salt between them to the king. Special salt roads were used to transport the precious commodity to the main urban centres; these tended to bypass settlements on the route in order to avoid paying local tolls.

The town's burgesses were involved in trade, craft and industry, and specialist guilds were beginning to emerge. In 1196 there were some fifteen bakers in Leicester, serving a population of about two thousand; they were obliged to grind their corn at the lord's mill and to use the lord's ovens to bake their bread. From about 1150 bakers formed guilds in an effort to protect them from manorial lords, and in 1155 London bakers formed a brotherhood. Among the crafts were groups of goldsmiths and leatherworkers, while among the trades were groups of bakers, shoemakers, butchers and fishmongers. Weavers, fullers and dyers were particular important in places like

Jews House, Lincoln. A twelfth-century merchants' house with shops on the ground floor.

York and Lincoln; poorer-quality cloths such as russet and burrel were already being exported in the twelfth century.

In the borough, merchants, tradesmen and craftsmen lived closely together. Houses on narrow plots ran back from the high street, with gardens and outbuildings. Although this accommodation was often cramped and unsanitary, and the burgesses owed services and taxes to their lord, they tended to have more status and wealth than the rural population. Most town houses were built of timber, and fire was a constant hazard. Some stone houses, belonging to goldsmiths and financiers, were constructed in the twelfth century. By 1200 there were more than thirty stone houses in Canterbury, where the elite dwelled.

External latrines, often called 'privies', were built as far away from the house as possible, often over a river or stream. Cesspits were lined with wood or stone and cleared out periodically. The contents of cesspits would be 'sweetened' by the regular deposition of a straw layer on top of the waste. Urinal pots were used in town houses.

Water in towns was unfit to drink unless heated in the process of brewing. Sanitary conditions in towns were poor and life expectancy for many was shorter even than in the countryside. Rickets and joint disorders were endemic.

FOOD AND DRINK

IN ARISTOCRATIC HOUSEHOLDS there were two principal meals: dinner which would be have been taken mid-morning and the second, supper which was taken about 4p.m. Meals were eaten in the great hall. The extravagance of medieval royal feasts is notorious. We don't have the precise details of twelfth-century royal banquets, but we know that vast quantities of meat and game were consumed, including pork, mutton, venison, wild duck, capons, wild boar, cranes, geese, swans and peppered peacocks. Elaborate planning went into the preparations for coronation and royal marriage feasts. Animals were bought at summer fairs and specially fattened for such occasions; additionally thousands of hens, game birds and rabbits were ordered months before the event. For example 1,900 chickens were purchased in Kent in 1189 for Richard I's coronation feast. Thousands of gallons of wine were ordered in the summer and rice, almonds and sugar two months before the feast. Considerable importance was placed on good table manners for young men who served or ate at table in noble households. Royal and baronial tables were covered with cloth and the servers who handled the wine cup carried napkins.

Wheat bread was eaten by the aristocracy, with rye and barley bread for the peasantry; but there was also a regional division, reflecting the predominance of wheat in the south and other cereals further north and east. The bread was unleavened and served in the form of flat cakes. A *manchet* was a 2-pound best quality loaf. Only a few peasant households had their own bread oven and most would have relied on a communal village oven.

At the table there were dishes for meat and fish; some meat was served on spits, as portrayed on the Bayeux Tapestry. Knives were used, sometimes one shared between two diners, but no forks. Trenchers, thick slices of stale bread with a little of the centre scooped out, were often used instead of plates. After the meal they were given to the 'lower' members of the household. Wooden trenchers were used by peasants.

Opposite:
The medieval kitchen in Dover Castle, with a range of copper and ceramic vessels.

A poem read in grammar schools warned:

Never eat bread with abandon till
they have set down the dishes;
People may think you are famished,
else they may judge you a glutton.
Tidy the nails of your fingers – dirt
to your friends is offensive.
Eat what is served as your portion,
send what is left to the needy.
Relish such talk as is peaceful; try not
to chatter when speaking,
Nor let your laughter be raucous …
('O Boy standing at the table',
attrib. Bishop Grosseteste, d.1253)

The interior of the great hall at Chepstow Castle. It was built by William fitz Osbern who was made Earl Palatinate of Hereford within a few months of the Battle of Hastings. Chepstow is the earliest known stone castle in Britain and was built along the lines of the fortified palaces found in pre-Conquest Normandy.

Pork, mutton and beef were the main meats eaten four days a week, with fish served on Wednesdays, Fridays and Saturdays. During Lent fish would replace meat entirely and fish also played a large role in banquets, where it could be baked in pies, made into jellies or carved as roasts. A wide variety of sea fish were eaten, including mackerel, hake, haddock, herring and conger eels. Freshwater fish such as trout, carp and tench would also have been available from fishponds located on manors throughout the country. In 1086 the manor of Sandwich (Kent) paid 40,000 herrings in rent to Christ Church, Canterbury.

Cooking for the feast on the eve of the Battle of Hastings, as depicted on the Bayeaux Tapestry. Meat is being served on skewers.

Shellfish were also commonly consumed, including mussels, cockles and whelks. Oysters were particularly popular in monasteries and thick layers of oyster shells have been found during archaeological excavations at the Cistercian monasteries at Bordesley Abbey (Worcs) and Fountains Abbey (North Yorkshire). Some manors kept large stocks of salt for home curing. The Normans introduced new varieties of apples (and cider); in the twelfth century returning crusaders brought citrus fruits, pomegranates and spices to England from the

A table laid for a meal, from the mid-twelfth-century *The Littlemore Anselm.* (MS. Auct. D. 2. 6, 186v)

Middle East. Dried fruits also came from the Mediterranean and were considered medicinally better than fresh fruit. Herbs were widely used and a later medieval inventory lists over one hundred different varieties necessary in the kitchen garden. Meat and fish dishes were flavoured with ginger, cinnamon, nutmeg and cloves. Sugar from sugar cane was also introduced at this time.

Another consequence of the crusades was the introduction of sweet wines from southern Europe and the eastern Mediterranean. These became very popular as they supplemented the rather sour wines produced in England and northern France. Under the Plantagenet kings, Burgundy, claret and other wines were imported in increasingly large volumes at the expense of domestic wine. Mead, made from honey, was a popular drink at the tables of the aristocracy.

The peasant day started off with bread and ale, with bread and cheese or onion at midday, and the main meal in the evening would have been bread, soup or pottage. Pottage, consisting of pulped vegetables, oatmeal, salt and herbs, was eaten by all peasants, and broths with pieces of toasted bread were also common. On special occasions poultry, hare or salt beef might have found their way into the pot. The basic peasant diet contained a high level of carbohydrate in the form of grain, mainly barley and oats, baked into bread or brewed into ale. Meat and eggs for protein were in shorter supply, which meant many meat-free days. Some better-off peasant women made cheese and butter, but even salted fish would have been rare in many households. Large quantities of bacon were eaten, even by the poorest, as many country dwellers kept a pig. In the peasant household, animals not required for the next year would be killed in the autumn and the

Calendar from
St Albans, c. 1140,
showing the
November task
of killing the pig
for curing and
providing winter
protein. (MS.
Auct. D. 2. 6, 6v)

meat salted for use throughout the winter. Salt meat and fish would form an important source of protein throughout the winter months.

Cooking was carried out on a central hearth in the living room, often using a ubiquitous earthenware cooking pot which was either suspended from the roof or sat on a metal tripod over the fire. Heated pebbles dropped into a cooking pot (known as pot boilers) were sometimes used as an alternative to cooking directly on a fire and have been found on some rural sites. There would have been fruit and vegetables, onions, peas and beans, grown in the family's own garden. Poorer peasants ate soup or vegetables without meat, or perhaps bacon rind and beans. After poor harvests, bread made from bean flour and wheat sievings was eaten.

Those working for a lord on certain tasks would be fed for the duration of their employment. Those craftsmen involved in the building trade, such as thatchers, could expect a higher bread ration than their counterparts. Tenants involved in ploughing or harvesting were also rewarded with better food. At harvest time the first dinner consisted of soup, wheat bread, beef, cheese and as much ale as the workers wanted. At the end of the twelfth century a generous abbot of Titchfield provided flesh or fish, together with bread, ale or cider and broth. For supper the tenants were given a meal of a fish and a wheaten or barley loaf of 40 ounces. At Christmas it was the custom for tenants to give the lord a hen and at Easter, eggs, in return for being allowed to keep poultry.

Ale was the most common peasants' drink and was consumed in large quantities. Its alcohol content was quite low and it consisted of malted barley, water and yeast. It was cloudy, full of carbohydrate and protein, providing an additional source of nutrition. Brewing ale was normally

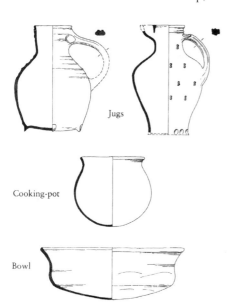

Jugs

Cooking-pot

Bowl

Early medieval pottery vessels, including a cooking pot of the type found in every peasant's home.

women's work, and often ale-wives would sell their surplus produce. Ale houses developed in this way and in early thirteenth-century Wakefield almost all the recorded brewers were women.

The poorest in society drank water, which in towns could be heavily polluted. This was known as a 'dry boon'. When ale, or sometimes cider, was provided it was known as a 'wet boon'.

Janus figure sitting on a claw-footed stool before a large cooking pan on a hearth. Detail of January from English calendar c. 1150. (MS. Bodl. 614, 3r)

Regular foods were supplemented by birds and rabbits caught in the woods or on the common. Honey taken from hives kept in the croft or on the common was used as a sweetener. Some tenants could pay to fish in manorial waters, while a number of lords provided 'common water' to fish in. Poaching of deer, fish and game birds was common and fines for offences regularly appear in manorial court records.

Although towns were not self-sufficient, townsmen tended to enjoy a wider choice of food than country dwellers. By 1200 many manors around London were already providing for the capital's needs. Grain, live cattle, fresh meat, fresh poultry and even bread were all brought in on a daily basis. Pigs and cows were often raised in the city; there was, for instance, a piggery at Westminster Abbey which sold surplus animals on the open market. Cheese and butter were imported from Suffolk and Essex. A wide variety of vegetables and fruit were grown in city gardens and were also imported. The wealthy townsman could enjoy delicacies such as quinces, peaches, mulberries and medlars.

Specialised regular markets were established in London and other towns. Meat was chiefly sold at the 'Stokkes', roughly on the site of the Mansion House, while fish was sold in Eastcheap and Old Fish Street. General foods such as poultry, cheese, herbs and fruit were sold in Gracechurch Street and Cornhill, while Leadenhall market sold grain. The town authorities regulated the markets – hours, prices, quality, and weights and measures.

Along the banks of the Thames there was a concentration of cookshops that sold ready-prepared food. This included roast thrush and finches as well as goose, chicken and capon baked in pastry, pies, soups and stews. They seem to have originally supplied meals directly to customers' houses as many homes had no adequate kitchen or cooking facilities, but later provided meals on a takeaway basis. In 1212 it was ordered that the cookshops should be whitewashed and plastered and have no internal partitions in order to prevent fire.

Overleaf: Artist's reconstruction of a meal taken in a Norman baronial hall. The lord, his wife and honoured guests sit at the high table and are served first. Other visitors, knights and senior household officials are at the side tables. The amounts of food served would have diminished further away from the lord a diner was sat. The tables have linen table-cloths, but there are few eating utensils. Musicians are entertaining the diners from the upstairs gallery. The great hall was lit by rush and animal-fat torches.

Shopping and Style

Y THE LATE TWELFTH CENTURY hundreds of markets had been
created. For example, in 1086 there were only two markets in
Oxfordshire; by 1200 there were at least ten. Everyone was within
walking distance (10 miles) of weekly markets, which were held on
different days of the week, allowing traders to establish a circuit of
permanent business. In the early twelfth century Sunday was a
favourite market day and markets were often held in churchyards.
Eventually Sunday markets were prohibited by the Church and
dedicated open market areas were created in town and village centres.

The markets served the needs of craftsmen, farmers and landlords
of the region. Some were held in towns specifically created in order
to attract trade. Witney (Oxfordshire), for instance, was founded by
the bishops of Winchester *c*. 1180. The large triangular open area
which distinguishes the centre was designed to accommodate a large
livestock as well as a produce market. The narrow market entrances,
equipped with toll gates, ensured that traders would be taxed on their
goods.

A town with a market aspired to an annual fair as well. Bishop
Walkelin of Winchester obtained a licence from William II for a three-
day St Giles fair in the town, which was so successful that it generated
sufficient funds to complete the building of his cathedral. In order to
protect the fair's business, all trading in Winchester and for miles
around was forbidden for the duration of the fair. In addition to cloth,
wool and hides from northern England, horses, tin and lead from the
West Country were traded. Merchants from Spain, Provence, Ghent,
Bruges and Italy brought spices and silks, woad, wine, 'best' iron, fine
textiles, madder and brassware. 'Strange' beasts and birds, apes, bears
and ferrets were also brought for sale here.

Special rules were applied to large gatherings of strangers where
money and drink were plentiful. Henry I granted the bishop of
Norwich permission to extend the length of fairs in Norwich, Lynn

Opposite:
Shepherds
dressed in
peasant clothes
from a twelfth-
century psalter.
(MS. Douce 293,
9r)

and Hoxne and extended protection to those going to or coming from them, recognising that fairs could lead to riotous behaviour.

The term *schopa* (shop) was used for a workshop throughout the Middle Ages, since many craftsmen made and sold their wares in the same place. In most small towns shops probably started as market stalls in front of the residence where a craftsman or butcher lived and worked. Over time the stalls became permanent buildings as they were roofed and integrated into the main building. The Norman House in Lincoln has an undercroft, and a row of shops on the ground floor. Such shops had no access to the rest of the building and were leased to traders. Shops opened at dawn and closed in the afternoon. Some rows of shops or stalls were dedicated to specific groups of traders; in particular, butchers commonly had their 'shambles' segregated to keep their smells and debris away from other retailers and shoppers.

Throughout the period the only coin minted was the silver penny, known as the *denarius* (hence, $1d. = 1$ penny). By 1200, four million pennies a year were being minted. Even so, peasants only used coins at market and for rents. Excavations of village houses produce few coins, partly because they were valued and thus rarely mislaid. If smaller denominations were required, coins were cut into half-pennies and farthings.

The punishment for counterfeiting was severe. In 1124 the silver pennies shipped to Normandy to pay for Henry I's troops were well below the required standard and in response the king:

Battle Abbey and town. Before the battle of Hastings William vowed to build an abbey on the battlefield if he was successful. He placed the high altar on the spot where Harold died.

commanded that all the moneyers ... in England should be [punished], because a pound would not buy a penny's worth at market. Bishop Roger of Salisbury sent all over England and commanded them all to come to Winchester at Christmas. There they came and they took them, one by one, and deprived them of their right hands and testicles. (*Anglo-Saxon Chronicle*, 1125)

A silver penny of William the Conqueror.

The use of only one denomination of coin caused problems of transport as huge numbers of pennies had to be collected and moved around the kingdom. Shire reeves had the problem of transporting over 100 pounds weight of pennies to the king every year. In 1194 Ralph of Cornhill paid three shillings to buy six casks 'to bring pennies to the lord king'.

In 1130 the royal court was able to acquire luxury items including taffeta, satin, towels and linen, herrings, oil, nuts, wine, pepper, cumin and ginger. By 1200 there were many small luxuries that added to the elegance of dress. A French song describing the wares of a travelling merchant mentions girdles and gloves, pins and needles, linen kerchiefs with flowers and birds embroidered on them, and saffron wimples. He also sold ladies' toilet aids, which included 'razors, tweezers, looking glasses, tooth-brushes, bandeaus and curling irons, ribbons, combs, mirrors, rose-water ... cotton with which they rouge, and whitening ...'

Elegant gloves of lamb, rabbit or fox skin were often given as presents. Jewellery added to noble women's adornment; the most common item was a gold ring, which might have incorporated a diamond, emerald or sapphire. The ring brooch was another fashionable item, normally made of gold or silver and decorated with stones and inscriptions.

The shaved heads of Norman messengers, from the Bayeux Tapestry.

Although civilian dress was much the same for both Normans and English of the same social class, dress was an indicator of status. After the Conquest the cloaks worn by the upper classes were long, trailing to the ground. Henry II, nicknamed Curtmantle (short cloak), introduced the short cloak from Anjou. Court styles could be outlandish: William II introduced a fashion for shoes with long curving toes

like rams' horns. Normal footwear was a soft leather slipper, with no reinforcement of the sole, although peasants might have wooden soles for outdoor work. Sleeves hanging down to the knees were an aristocratic fashion for women throughout the period. Necklines in the form of a short split, fastened with a brooch, were common to women's dresses and men's tunics.

For the aristocracy, fur was a mark of opulence and the king used sable and ermine, the most expensive varieties, for his robes and bedspread. The least expensive furs were lamb and cat, and these were worn to demonstrate spirituality by churchmen such as Bishop Wulfstan of Worcester, who wore only lambskin. He claimed that men of worldly wisdom could wear the skins of cunning animals, but that he was an innocent soul and content with innocent lamb.

Peasants wore wide-bottomed leather or woollen breeches (*braies*), woollen tunics or doublets worn over a shirt, and a coarse woollen cloak. The tunic was confined by a belt at the waist, to which a knife, purse (*gypcire*) and tools might be attached. In winter they wore a coarse woollen cap or hood. This was a simple cowl with a point at the back, pulled on over the head, with sufficient cloth to protect the neck and shoulders. Peasant women wore similar clothes to their menfolk, but without the braies. Their tunics were long and girdled around the waist and their sleeves were wide and flowing.

The Bayeux Tapestry portrays clean-shaven Normans, with their hair cropped on the back of their heads, in contrast to the longer-haired Anglo-Saxons, who also wore moustaches. For about a century after 1066 long hair continued to distinguish Englishmen from Normans. When William II and Henry I and their courts wore their hair long they drew accusations of effeteness and the bishop of Sées denounced Henry I's courtiers for wearing their hair like women. Archbishop Anselm observed:

Those who are unwilling to have a hair-cut may not enter church; if they do … the priest … should announce to them that they enter against God's will and to their own damnation.

The martyrdom of Thomas Becket. The Archbishop and priest are shown with tonsured heads. The knights are led by Reginald fitz Urse. c. 1220.

Women wore their hair longer than men. Unmarried women wore it loose, while married women wore it bound or braided. As the cowl was not yet universally worn by clerics, they were visibly distinguished from other men by their tonsure and their shaven face. Ecclesiastical rulings of the period declared that the clerk's tonsure or 'crown' should be clear and visible. The beard was worn in full at the beginning of the twelfth century but was gradually modified until, by the end of the century, it had virtually disappeared, apart from in rural areas and among the elderly. However, shaving was still fairly primitive and most men would have had a stubble.

A twelfth-century partly glazed ceramic chamber pot.

Bone and antler combs have been found in York and Winchester, where there were comb-making craftsmen. Such accessories are associated with Scandinavian influence. John of Wallingford (*d*.1214) claimed that 'the Danes, thanks to their habit of combing their hair every day, of bathing every Saturday and regularly changing their clothes, were able to undermine the virtue of married women and even seduce the daughters of nobles to be their mistresses'.

According to Lanfranc, washing and bodily cleanliness were not high priorities; he suggests that monks bathed only three times a year, at Christmas, Easter and Whitsun. More probably monks were reasonably fastidious, as there was a *lavatorium* (wash basin with running water) in the cloister close to the refectory, for washing hands before and after meals. There were dedicated bathrooms and latrines (garderobes) served with water in royal palaces, but most households' idea of luxury would have been a chamber pot.

The Norman *lavatorium* in the cloisters at Wenlock Priory, Shropshire, used by monks to wash before taking meals. The carved panel is one of two surviving examples here of a fine regional carving style.

51

sup lift. magnificentia

rabilis ds in scis suis: d

eni in altitudine maris:

aboraui damans rauce

TRANSPORT AND TRAVEL

NUMEROUS TRAVELLERS MOVED ALONG THE ROADS of twelfth-century England. Some were on business: knights with their followers, answering their lord's summons; manorial officials driving cattle or sheep for use at another establishment; or royal huntsmen bringing deer to stock the park of a favoured baron. Other travellers, both lay and religious, combined pilgrimage with the desire to see new places. The roads were worn by the passage of goods. There were packhorses, driven by grooms and laden with almost every variety of merchandise, and slow-moving carts. The Norman era was characterised by extensive building projects requiring timber, stone and lime, and although it was cheaper to transport heavy goods by water, many places were not served by rivers, therefore much building material was carried by road at considerable expense.

Royalty, bishops and the higher aristocracy were constantly on the move. They had property scattered across the country and would regularly move from one castle or estate to another. Business, pleasure or ceremony in the form of royal councils, ecclesiastical assemblies, hunting, tournaments, church dedications, pilgrimage and crusade all involved travel. In the early twelfth century Eadmer, a Canterbury monk, explained that his master, Archbishop Anselm, was always on the move because it was custom but it was also a means of supervising his scattered estates. It also meant that it saved transporting produce to Canterbury, as the prelate's household could instead be accommodated and fed as it moved around the country. Some royal estates were even assessed in units of 'one night's provisions'.

Even peasants and lowly freemen would travel to the local weekly market, which could be up to 10 miles away. They would visit the annual fairs and might even go on pilgrimage. A few would have been involved in warfare in France or further afield on crusade. The spread of small exotic artefacts to remote rural areas indicates contact with if not actual travel to many remote parts of the world.

Opposite:
A capital 'S' decorated with a sailing boat, from an English psalter, c. 1200. (MS. Gough Liturg. 2, 82r)

Horse and cart
from a
thirteenth-
century French
manuscript. (MS.
Douce 48, 18v)

It has been estimated that King John's court moved fourteen times a month, and as a consequence his retinue rarely slept in the same place for more than two or three consecutive nights. The king's household was essentially portable and individual servants such as 'the bearer of the king's bed' and 'the serjeant of the buttery' had their own packhorses. The logistics of such an operation were complex and required detailed forward planning; thus two of the king's bakers always went ahead to prepare bread at his next destination. The royal accounts (pipe rolls) record continuous expenditure on saddle bags, panniers and halters for the packhorses and harness and cart covers for wagons. For example, in 1207 King John purchased 'a packhorse saddle with girth, reins and halter to transport our chapel' in Winchester. The Crown ensured that there were sufficient

Shoeing a horse
from a treatise
on the care of
horses, c. 1200. In
1198 the Crown
ordered 90,000
horseshoes from
the Forest of
Dean alone. (MS.
Douce 88, 51r)

supplies of wine scattered around the country for the use of the court. An audit of the king's wine in 1201 recorded that there were over seven hundred tuns (casks containing 252 gallons) of wine, much of it stored in fifteen royal castles and houses. It cost six shillings for the bishop of Winchester to move a tun of wine from Southampton to Witney in 1208.

The royal court spent most of its time travelling between its favourite destinations such as Westminster, Winchester, Woodstock and Gloucester. King John's itinerary for May 1209 was typical of a monarch's movements during the twelfth century. On Friday 8 May the court was at Gloucester and over the next three weeks it travelled 170 miles, visiting:

Sunday 10 May	Bristol
Wednesday 13 May	Bath
Thursday 14 May	Bath
Saturday 16 May	Marlborough
Sunday 17 May (Whitsun)	Marlborough
Monday 18 May	Marlborough
	Ludgershall
Wednesday 20 May	Winchester
Friday 22 May	Winchester
	Southampton

Anselm, Archbishop of Canterbury (1093–1109), who held estates scattered across southern England. (MS. Auct. D. 2. 6, 156r)

Preparations for the conquest of England, from the Bayeux Tapestry. Small and large wars would have involved the marshalling and movement of ordnance and armies throughout the Norman era.

Saturday 23 May	Southampton
Sunday 24 May (Trinity Sunday)	Portchester
Wednesday 27 May	Aldingbourne (Sussex)
Thursday 28 May	Arundel
	Bramber
	Knepp (Sussex)
Friday 29 May	Knepp

The distance travelled each day was limited by the speed of the carts carrying heavy equipment, and they could only go twelve to fifteen miles a day. In summer a household could move more rapidly; in the thirteenth century the countess of Leicester with her retinue was able to cover up to thirty miles a day.

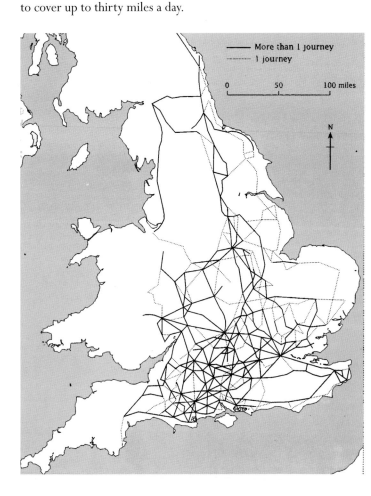

King John's journeys in England.

In 1158 Thomas Becket, then Henry II's chancellor, was sent on a mission to Paris. His retinue consisted of two hundred horsemen – knights, clerks, stewards, squires and the sons of nobles. There were eight wagons, each drawn by five great horses; two of the wagons carried barrels of top-quality beer. The chapel, chamber, store and kitchen each had its own wagon, while the remainder carried food, drink, tapestries and bedding. Twelve packhorses bore the chancellor's gold and silver plate, his money, clothes and the sacred vessels and books for the chapel. Tied to each wagon was a hunting dog and sitting on the back of each packhorse was a monkey. As the retinue entered the villages and fortresses of northern France, the 250 footmen in the van sang English songs. The hounds, hunt servants and wagons followed, then the packhorses, squires with their masters' shields, horses and falcons, then the household officials, followed by knights and clerks, riding two by two, and finally Becket and his close friends.

The royal household included a number of permanent messengers, who acted as low-level diplomats and kept the wheels

Lower Icknield Street runs along the northern scarp of the Chilterns. William and his army took this route on their way to his coronation in 1066.

of government turning. They were provided with horses, given their yearly robes and shoes, and were ranked above grooms. Royal and aristocratic households employed a marshal, who was in charge of horses, carts, wagons and the transporting of goods. Lower down the social scale, marshals also acted as farriers.

The four principal long-distance routes in Norman England, which originated in the Romano-British era, were Ermine Street or the Great North Road, the Foss Way from Lincoln to south-west England, Icknield Street from East Anglia to Wiltshire, and Watling Street from Dover to Chester and beyond. These routes had royal protection and in 1118 Henry I ruled that a 'royal way' should be wide enough for two wagons to pass each other, or sixteen knights to ride abreast. There are frequent references to the cutting back of trees and brushwood from the roadside to protect travellers from robbers. In addition the whole country was covered by a network of lesser tracks, droveways and paths. Most roads would not have been surfaced. Only in towns like Lincoln or Southampton would the streets have been paved or, as at Winchester, given a flint surface. On the whole, country roads were in a poor condition and it was a constant battle to keep them passable. Holes in the road and thick mud were the major problems. Main routes were very wide, up to a quarter of a mile in places, which allowed alternative tracks to be taken in bad weather.

Horsemen were the fastest travellers and could manage up to twenty-five miles a day. It took seven or eight days for the news of Becket's murder on 29 December 1170 to reach Devon, a distance of about 200 miles. Packhorses and carts could manage only about twelve miles a day. Travel was limited in winter, both by fewer daylight hours and by problems with flooding and frost. In the countryside a maze of tracks served the village and its fields, allowing access to the scattered strips within the open fields, and to meadows and pastures, commonland and woodland.

In the twelfth century one aspect of travel was improved significantly when stone bridges were built to replace either a wooden predecessor or a ford. At Durham, which had been virtually on an island, 'an arching stone bridge of wonderful workmanship' was built by Bishop Ranulf Flambard *c.* 1120. Another bridge, the Elvet, was built by a later bishop, Hugh de Puiset (1153–95). At Oxford a stone causeway was built across the Thames floodplain to the south of the city. The Grandpont, as it was called, was almost a mile long and improved access to Oxford considerably. The wooden London Bridge, the only bridge across the Thames, was rebuilt in stone by Peter,

chaplain of St Mary Colechurch, starting in 1176. When he died it was sufficiently complete for him to be interred in the chapel on the bridge.

Where possible, heavy goods would be carried by water and both sea and river ports were important in Norman England. York Minster was built with stone brought by river, then carried by sleds to the masons' yard. At Norwich, a short section of canal was built from the River Wensum to carry building materials to the site of the new cathedral. Henry I re-cut part of the Foss Dyke between the rivers Witham and Trent in order to speed transport with the north. The tidal Thames was also used when possible, and those travelling from London to Canterbury or the Kent ports would do so regularly by river as far as Gravesend.

Wine was carried from London on the Thames to the river port of Henley and then transported overland by cart to Woodstock Palace. In return, grain from the bishop of Winchester's estates was loaded on to barges at Henley and shipped downstream to London. By 1205 a system of river tolls had been established between Oxford and London.

The largely unaltered medieval Newbridge between Abingdon and Witney, Oxfordshire. It was built on the orders of King John to improve communications for the wool trade and is claimed to be the oldest surviving bridge across the River Thames.

RELAXATION AND ENTERTAINMENT

THERE WAS ONLY A NARROW DIVIDE between spiritual and secular in the area of entertainment in Norman England, and most medieval music and drama developed out of church liturgy. The main musical activity of monasteries, cathedrals and great minsters was chant, but surprisingly little liturgical music survives from this period. In the late twelfth century the Cambridge Songbook appeared, containing Latin songs which were sung at intervals in the chant. Organs were probably in general use, at least in monastic churches, by the mid-twelfth century. Polyphony was developing at this time and Abbot Aelred of Rievaulx (1109–66) regretted that the common people admired the sound of organs, the noise of cymbals and harmony with pipes and cornet, in preference to plain chant. The little vernacular music which survives all has a religious theme and includes a crusading song in Norman French, *Parti de Mal* (c. 1200), and three short pieces by the hermit Godric of Finchale (d. 1170).

Virtually nothing remains of the non-religious songs and music of the period, although occasional references convey a distant echo of that lost world of song. Harps, viols and zithers are depicted in contemporary carvings and pictures, as are various kinds of horn. There are references to girls and women singing the songs of the hero Hereward. Although some prelates like Bishop Robert of Hereford (1131–48) spurned 'singers and actors', there was no barrier between secular and ecclesiastical melodies. Thomas, archbishop of York (1070–1100), was adept at bridging these worlds: 'he was powerful in voice and chant and composed many religious songs. If a minstrel sang in his hearing, he would immediately transform what he heard into divine praise.' Gerald Cambriensis tells that when Gilbert of Clare was travelling to his estates in south Wales, he was preceded by a minstrel and a singing man, who played and sang alternately. Among the instruments played by minstrels were viols, cytherns (mandolin-type instruments), drums, cymbals and harps. Harpists were highly

Opposite:
Man juggling, from an eleventh-century French manuscript.

61

Men playing bells
and a form of
harp, c. 1180. (MS.
Auct. D. 2. 8, 88r)

Mummers and
dancers, Flemish
manuscript. (MS.
Bodl. 264, pt. I,
21v)

regarded and in 1183 the earl of Gloucester rewarded his harper with a grant of land in Bristol in return for the nominal rent of a dish of beans on St John's Day.

It was the custom to dance in the churchyard on the eve of the local saint's feast day and Reginald of Durham (*fl.* 1162–73) tells of how the population gathered at St Cuthbert's Chapel on St Cuthbert's Day, the elders praying inside the church, the younger, 'as is the custom of youth', singing and dancing outside. At Burton Fleming (East Riding, Yorkshire) 'when the clergy and congregation had left the church and locked the door, the younger men, girls and boys played and joked and danced in the green space of the churchyard'. The Church authorities were not happy with such festivity and in the early thirteenth century prohibitions were issued against dancing and 'lascivious games in churches and churchyards'. The Church was more relaxed about drama, seeing it as an extension of the visual teaching methods found in frescoes and sculpture. These were the basic tools of religious education for a non-literate congregation. Liturgy and drama had overlapped since before the Conquest, particularly at Easter. An account of Easter at Eynsham Abbey (Oxfordshire) in the 1190s tells how every year

there is a dramatic representation of the Lord's resurrection. First there is the revelation by the angel, addressing the women at the sepulchre, who tells them of the triumph of their king and how they must inform the disciples. Then there is an enactment of Christ's appearance in the form of a gardener to his beloved Mary [Magdalene].

Miracle plays based on saints' lives were performed from the early twelfth century. Writing in 1173–4 William fitz Stephen declared that 'London has holier plays', depicting the lives of the confessors and the deaths of martyrs. The *Play of Adam* is a surviving twelfth-century drama, probably written and performed in England. This deals with the Fall and the story of Cain and Abel, concluding with a procession of prophets. It was designed to be performed outside a church with a choir to sing passages from the Bible at appropriate points.

Many of the entertainments associated with the later Middle Ages were already enjoyed by the twelfth century. The king, barons and bishops all had resident minstrels, and there were jesters and puppet shows at court as well. The Earl of Hereford's jester was called *Folebarba*, 'crazy beard', while Henry II's jester was known as 'Roland the Farter', who every Christmas, 'used to leap, whistle and fart before the king'. Some of these entertainers achieved considerable wealth. For example, Rahere, Henry I's minstrel, founded St Bartholomew's Priory and Hospital at Smithfield in 1123. Other entertainers moved from place to place, feast to feast and market to market. These included jugglers, acrobats, owners of performing bears and tellers of funny and lewd stories. The Church denounced them as ribalds and lechers, but they were mostly welcomed by the laity, for whom non-pious and non-judgemental entertainment of this sort would probably have been welcome.

Even indoor board games could have a religious theme. *Alea Evangelii*, 'the game of the gospels', was based on an earlier Scandinavian game, but a twelfth-century manuscript at Corpus Christi, Oxford describes the layout of the board as a religious allegory. Nine Men's Morris was a board game with even older roots. It is a form of chequers and there are boards carved into the early medieval cloister seats at several English cathedrals, including Canterbury and Gloucester, presumably to entertain monks between services. Chess and tables (a form of backgammon) were also played in the twelfth century. According to Reginald of Durham, a craftsman from Kirkcudbright made chessmen, draughts and dice out of walrus tusks,

Middle English secular poem set to music, thirteenth century. (MS. Rawl. G. 18, 105v)

The Lewis chessmen, carved from walrus ivory and whales' teeth, 1150–1200.

A couple playing Nine Men's Morris, from a Flemish manuscript of the *Romance of Alexander*. (MS. Bodl. 264, pt.I, 112r)

er   6 adifer a troube: 7 bens rofte foi
uus landj   Q uant li valles les uit/si demande poe quoi
nauer   J lles a tant laisses/biau nies fait il p foi
iher   E n secours wus amaine/alixand' le roi
her   D emain sera losies/gtremont ce rochoi

bone and jet. Ninety-three chess pieces made from walrus ivory and whales' teeth and dating from 1150 to 1200 were found on the Isle of Lewis in 1831. They appear to have been made in Norway and it has been suggested that they could have been used to play games other than chess. Another ancient game, associated with gambling, was dicing, which could lead to distressing losses as described in this contemporary poem:

Twelfth-century bone skates from London.

> In the second place I own
> To the vice of gaming:
> Cold indeed outside I seem.
> Yet my soul is flaming:
> But when once the dice-box hath
> Stripped me to my shaming,
> Make I songs and verses fit
> For the world's acclaiming.
> (Archpoet, 'The Confession of Golias', *c.* 1160)

William fitz Stephen (*d.* 1191) was a servant of Thomas Becket who witnessed his murder and wrote his biography. He also wrote an account of London in the twelfth century which included sections on the capital's pastimes and sporting activity. He noted that on Shrove Tuesday 'boys bring fighting cocks to their schoolmaster, and the entire morning is given over to boyish sport'. He continues, 'after lunch all the youth of the city go out into the fields to take part in a ball game', which appears to have been an early form of football, witnessed by 'older citizens, fathers and wealthy citizens, who come on horseback to watch their juniors competing'.

Fitz Stephen also described impromptu horseracing at Smithfield, and combat where aspirants for knighthood entered into mock battle, armed with lance and shield, with the sons of London's citizens. At Easter there were sports on the Thames, where there was a shield fixed to a mast in mid-river and 'a young man standing in the prow of a small boat, propelled by the current and several rowers, has to strike shield with a lance'. When the marshes to the north of London were frozen, lumps of ice were used as sledges and animal shin bones as skates.

Boys tilt at each other. One rides a donkey, the other a dog. From the *Romance of Alexander*. (MS. Bodl. 264, pt. I, 50r)

Fitz Stephen defined other summer games as archery, wrestling, javelin throwing, jumping and duelling with shields. On festival days in winter there was boar, bull and bear-baiting. In the countryside there would have been a range of other sports involving what would now be considered extreme cruelty to animals.

During the year the great Church festivals of Christmas and Easter together with harvest festivals provided cause for celebration. At Christmas, work often stopped for fourteen days and the lord would hold a feast. Each tenant would take a log, to guard against his portion being undercooked, a dish, a mug and a napkin. Often mummers' plays and exotic dances were performed on these occasions, bringing together the mixture of Christian, classical and pagan that characterised many aspects of everyday life in the twelfth century.

A man playing dice and drinking, French, c. 1300. (MS. Douce 308, 259r)

Walter Map noted that 'in each parish the English have a house for drinking' and communal drinking parties were held regularly. Gerald of Wales records a drinking competition between Henry II and monks at a Cistercian monastery. Heavy drinking at court could lead to quarrels and violence and the English had a reputation as drinkers. Richard fitz Neal believed that high levels of crime were explained 'by the drunkenness, which is inborn of the inhabitants'.

dixit i

ds̄. pꝛo

ducant

aque

reptile

amme

uiuen

ꞇuolati

le sup

tram: sub firmam̄to celi. ꞇcreauitq̄; ds̄ cete grandia
ꞇomnem animam uiuentem atq̄; motabilem quāp̄
dyxerant aque inspecies suas. ꞇomne uolatile secūm
genus suum. Et uidit ds̄ q̄ ēet bonum: bn̄dixitq̄; eis
dicens. Crescite ꞇmultiplicamini. ꞇreplete aquas ma
ris. auesq̄; multiplicentur sup̄ tram; Et factum. ē.
uespere ꞇmane dies quintus.

EDUCATION AND SCHOLARSHIP

Before 1066 Anglo-Saxon was the dominant spoken language in England, with a dialect of Anglo-Scandinavian spoken in the north. Following the Conquest, the king, barons, leading churchmen and the aristocracy, who had been born and brought up in northern France, spoke French; thus for several generations after 1066 French remained the vernacular language of the rulers. None of the Norman kings or their immediate successors spoke English. Ironically, by the second half of the twelfth century the French spoken in England was thought to be inferior to that spoken in the Paris region of France and became known as 'Marlborough French'. Aristocratic families began to 'send their sons to be brought up in France in order to be trained in arms and have the barbarity of their native language removed' (Gervase of Tilbury, c. 1150–c. 1228).

A large number of French words concerning literature, architecture and culture were 'adopted' into the English language. The language of commerce and trade was heavily influenced by Norman French, but at peasant level there was relatively little change. Beef (*boeuf*) replaced cow and mutton (*mouton*) replaced sheep as the flesh of those animals, but generally there was little borrowing of agricultural, industrial or fishing terms.

English remained the mother tongue of the vast majority of people in England after 1066, and even aristocratic Norman children were becoming fluent in English by the end of the eleventh century. In order to run the country efficiently, a large body of English speakers would have been needed, and by the mid-twelfth century most of the heirs of the original Norman conquerors and settlers would have been bilingual or exclusively spoken English.

Soon after the Conquest the tradition of issuing writs and laws in English stopped and the composition of poetry and religious works also soon ended, but the *Anglo-Saxon Chronicle* continued to be written in English at Peterborough Abbey until the reign of Henry II. By the

Opposite:
God creating beasts, from the Ashmole Bestiary, c. 1200.
(MS. Ashmole 1511, 6v)

end of the twelfth century, English was reviving. Significantly, the new version of English was somewhat different from the standard literary West Saxon in which earlier documents were written. The grammar was simpler and linguistic historians draw a line between the Old English of *Beowulf* and the Middle English of Chaucer in the Norman era. Nevertheless, an impressive body of French literature emerged from the Anglo-Norman world. For instance, the earliest manuscript of the French epic *Song of Roland*, called the Oxford manuscript, dates from the mid-twelfth century and comes from England, as does Philippe de Thaon's *Bestiary* (1121–35).

By far the largest body of written material produced in Norman England was in Latin. The richness and diversity of literature produced gives it a claim to be the greatest epoch of English Latin. A remarkable example is provided by Walter Map's *Courtiers' Trifles*, an assemblage of anecdotes, legends and sometimes barbed comments on contemporary life, especially that of the court and the monks.

Most inhabitants of Norman Britain were illiterate. Literacy was largely the preserve of the clergy, who used Latin to sing Mass, to say offices and to conduct the business of the Church. The story of Orderic Vitalis's education is typical of the early Norman era. Orderic was born near Shrewsbury in 1075 to an English mother and a Norman father, Odelerius of Orleans, who came to Shropshire as a clerical member of the house of the earl of Shrewsbury, Roger of Montgomery. At the age of five, Orderic was sent to study under a Saxon cleric, Siward, who served his father's church of St Peter (later Shrewsbury Abbey). Orderic seems to have learnt and spoken Latin, and from his time as a schoolboy in England acquired sympathy for the English cause, which is evident in his *Historia*

Shrewsbury Abbey was founded by the palatinate Earl Roger de Montgomery in 1083. It sits on the site of St Peter's where Orderic Vitalis was taught.

Ecclesia (Ecclesiastical History). When he was eleven, Orderic was sent as a novice to the abbey of Saint-Evroult in Normandy, where he completed his education.

The task of educating knights' sons might fall to a chaplain or a schoolteacher, known as a *magister* (master). Although by no means all knights were literate, they played an increasingly important part in local administration as their military role declined. They could be summoned to attend hundred and county courts, and they acted as coroners as well as tax collectors.

During the twelfth century a significant stimulus to the growth of schools in cathedrals, monasteries and minsters came from the need for a growing band of educated officials. The Crown,

The distribution of English schools in the twelfth century.

bishops, abbots and great landowners needed literate men for the conduct of their affairs in a society increasingly dependent on law, administration and taxation. Church schools admitted a number of boys who were not members of great households or members of religious houses, but wanted to be trained as parish clergy, parish clerks and literate laity. The admission of outsiders to Church schools would have been a way of doing favours and making money. Archbishop Lanfranc issued a charter for the canons of St Gregory, Canterbury (1085–7) to 'hold within the enclosure of the church, schools of grammar and music for the city and its villages'. It has been estimated that there were up to forty grammar schools in the country in the twelfth century, but such schools were often dependent on the interest and initiative of local priests or clerks.

A school could even be a source of profit, and there was competition over the right to run a school between two clerks of the bishop of Winchester: Jordan Fantosme, who ran the Winchester school opposite the cathedral, was in dispute with Master John Joichel. In London, St Paul's had a near-monopoly on

69

Two players from Terence's *Comedies*, twelfth-century manuscript from St Albans. Although such images were regularly copied in Norman England, the plays do not seem to have been performed at that time. (MS. Auct. F. 2. 13, 10r)

schooling, and the canons were instructed to excommunicate anyone 'who presumes to teach in the city of London without the permission of Henry, Master of the Schools, with the exception of those who run the schools of St Mary le Bow ['of the Arches'] and St Martin le Grand'. The Master of the Schools was a cathedral canon with his own endowment and the keys of the cathedral book cupboard.

We have no contemporary account of Norman schools, but we know that before the Conquest a group of boys at Aelfric Bata's school in southern England undertook a range of church duties similar to those of monks. They rose at midnight and joined the monks in church to say matins and then returned to bed. They rose again at dawn and the day was divided between schoolwork and services in church. The school was run by a monk-schoolmaster, who had an assistant. For writing they had wax tablets, styluses, penknives, rulers, ink and scraps of parchment and sat on benches. They also had individual copies of books and their homework included learning material to be sung in church. Badly behaved or lazy boys were beaten with a whip or rod. In *c.* 1170, the Durham monk Reginald wrote 'there is an ancient church dedicated to St Cuthbert, in which ... boys would at times devote themselves to study, stirred by the love of learning as well as

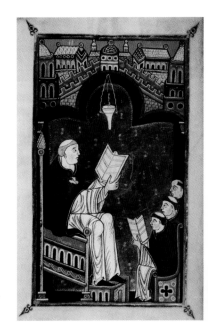

Right: Hugh of St Victor teaching a group of monks, twelfth-century manuscript from St Albans. (MS. Laud Misc. 409, 3v)

sometimes driven by fear of the blows of the fierce schoolmaster'.

Girls from an aristocratic background might undergo a similar education. Edward the Confessor's wife, Edith, spent part of her childhood with the nuns of Wilton Abbey (1030s and 1040s) where she learnt music, grammar and languages.

Pupils would have learnt Latin grammar through the fourth-century grammarian Donatus, who wrote the *Ars Minor* and more advanced *Ars Grammatica*. Later, an ideal curriculum recommended a wide range of authors. Having mastered the alphabet and Donatus, pupils moved on to learning Cato, Juvenal, Maximian, Horace and Ovid.

During the twelfth century new higher education institutions, known as 'schools', were developed. Notably, there were schools in Paris and Bologna, which attracted many Anglo-Norman students. For example, after receiving a basic grounding in Latin from a local priest, John of Salisbury went to Paris (1136). After twelve years of study he entered the service of the archbishop of Canterbury. Eventually he was appointed bishop of Chartres (1176–80), but his long education bore other fruit in the form of his writings, which are major monuments of twelfth-century humanist scholarship. His writings included the *Policraticus*, a blend of political theory and moral satire on the vices of court life.

Early seal of Oxford University.

Northampton, Exeter and Lincoln were all centres of higher education in the second half of the twelfth century, but by 1200 Oxford had emerged as the most important of the English schools, and a steady stream of scholars came to Oxford to study theology, law and medicine. Between 1190 and 1209 there were at least seventy masters in residence in the town. At this stage the university was not structured and students studied with individual masters, sharing living quarters in inns.

In 1187 Gerald of Wales gave a public reading of his new *Topography of Ireland* (*Topographia Hibernica*) in Oxford. He chose Oxford because 'that was the place in England where the clergy had flourished most'. He read the work on three successive days to different groups, including 'all the teachers of different subjects and the students of greater reputation and standing'.

prima cura ei : ad fiftulas.

Herbe Exifion de radice : uncias
·vi. Amili : uncias ·vi. Acetū : cya
thos duos · de adipe uulpis uncias tres
ᷓ in panno linies · ᷓ impones : mirabe
effectū bonum. Contᷓ capitis fractaᷓ.
Herbe Exifion superior pars sicca
ᷓ bene trita · ᷓ equis ponderibᷓ mi
xta · ᷓ capiti fracto apposita : de eo ossa
fracta extrahit. aut siquid in corpore so
poratum fuit. uel si pedibᷓ calcata sint
ossa alicui serpentis : eadem herba con
tra omnia uenena ualet. Nom iftī her
le Gallitricū aliud.

Prima   cura
ipsius   ad stru
mas uir   ginū.

Herba Gallitricum p se diligenter
trita. strumisᷓ uirginum impo
sita : eas pfectissime sanat. ad capillos
Herba Gallitricum trita. ungendos.
ᷓ cum oleo bene decocta : omnisᷓ
corpinis cum ea mixtis. pungas. capil
li nigri efficiuntur. si frequenti linie
ris.

Nom huᷓ
herbe :
Immo

Dec herba Immolū : clarissima
omnium ᷓ herbarum. homero at
cestante. ᷓ inuentore ipsius mercurio
assignante. que tussu cum beneficio de
monstratur. rotunda radice. ingraᷓ
in magnitudine. cepe est. ad dolorem
Herba Immolum con   matricis.
cusa · ᷓ imposita : dolorem matris
pfectissime sanat.

Homerus.   Mercurius.
          ducem.

Nom iftī herbe :
Eleotropiōᷓ. Dua
ᷓ maximas uirtutes habet.
Agrecis dicitur Eliorōᷓ. Alij : Dia
liton. Alij : Scorpion. Alij : Eraclea
uocant. Alij : Crouoferonᷓ ᷓ ropē
autē : Cinatres Galli : Uraſcorpī
Pyragoras : Hiſene. Egyptij : Ve
tamnū. Itali : oculeciam eā dic

MEDICINE AND
HEALING

MOST PEOPLE WHO BECAME SICK in Norman England had to rely on traditional remedies based on herbs, charms and prayer. Superstition, 'old wives' tales' and white magic were an integral and important element of everyday life, and spells and incantations were commonly tried to cure ailments. Most communities would have had a 'wise' man or woman with a reputation for identifying and curing disease. The use of herbs or gemstones was explained though the doctrine of 'signatures', which claimed that God had provided some form of remedy for every ill and that plants carried a signature upon them which indicated their usefulness. For instance, the seeds of skullcap, used as a headache remedy, appear to look like miniature skulls, while the white-spotted leaves of lungwort, used for tuberculosis, look like the lungs of a diseased patient. Most monasteries had herb gardens for herbal cures as well as for culinary use.

It was commonly believed that God sent illness as a punishment and that repentance could lead to recovery. Also, pilgrimage to shrines and sanctuaries was seen as the means of curing sickness. Relics of saints were much valued because of their supposed healing powers and provided a powerful attraction to the sick. After a vision of the Virgin Mary appeared at Walsingham in 1061 it became a centre of pilgrimage for the sick, and a visit to Our Lady of Walsingham involved taking the water, which was believed to have curative powers. Similarly, Bath, which had been a major shrine and healing centre in Roman Britain, was a popular centre for healing pilgrimage in Norman England. John of Villula, bishop of Bath and Wells (1088–1122), a wealthy physician before he became bishop, rebuilt the Romano-British bath complex here. In 1138 the *Gesta Stephani* described how 'from all over England sick people come to wash away their infirmities in the healing waters'. Miraculous cures here as elsewhere were broadcast widely in order to attract more visitors, which would result in increased endowments to the abbey. After the martyrdom of Becket there was considerable

Opposite: Medical and plant illustrations from a twelfth-century English Herbarium. (MS. Ashmole 1462, 26v)

rivalry between Canterbury and Bath as to which centre had the greater healing powers.

Professional physicians performed treatments such as bloodletting, trepanning and cauterisation, procedures which were often more dangerous than the disease. Gilbert of Sempringham reported that Lady Hawisa of Anwick (Lincs) had 'a red and swollen arm' for over a month after bloodletting and eventually sought the help of saints, the doctors having been so disastrous. According to William of Malmesbury, Edilina, wife of Richard the Saddler of Colleshill (Warwickshire), lost the use of her hand after a doctor had drawn blood from her thumb.

During the twelfth century new ideas about medicine came from the Muslim world. The Arab physician Ali al-Husayin's *Laws of Medicine*, translated into Latin at this time, deals with the formulation of medicines, diagnosis of disorders, general medicine and detailed therapies. In the twelfth century, Master Herbert the doctor donated twenty-six books on herbs, diseases and medicines to Durham Cathedral library, some translated from Arabic.

Charity provided some relief for those suffering from long-term illness or severe poverty, and in the century and a half after the Conquest hundreds of hospitals were founded. Treatment in hospital consisted of bed, warmth and a reasonable diet, perhaps supplemented by herbal remedies. At St Leonard's, York, ingredients for medicines, such as pepper and cumin, were bought for the infirmary, and Ospringe (Kent) bought almonds, pullets, milk and fresh goats' meat for the use of wealthy inmates. Conversely, sub-standard food found its way to some institutions; for instance, bread, ale, meat and fish judged unsound for sale was given to the leper hospital at Maldon (Essex).

A surgeon operating on polyps, twelfth-century English manuscript. (MS. Ashmole 1462, 10r)

Albule oculorum fic grea aunatur.

The term 'hospital' was also used for almshouses, which offered sheltered housing for the poor and elderly, and for hostels providing accommodation for pilgrims. Poor travellers could also expect hospitality from the hospitals in the form of up to three nights' stay and bread and ale as well as food for the onward journey. Such institutions became known as *Domus Dei* – 'God's House'. Archbishop Lanfranc founded a hospital at Canterbury *c*. 1077:

St Cross Hospital, Winchester, from a seventeenth-century etching.

He constructed a decent and ample house of stone beyond the north gate of the town and added to it many smaller dwellings [*habitacula*] for different human needs and conveniences, along with a spacious courtyard. He divided the main building into two, appointing one part for men oppressed by various kinds of infirmities and the other for women in a bad state of health. He also made arrangements for their clothing and daily food.

(Eadmer, *History of Recent Events in England*)

Inmates were accommodated under one roof with a chapel attached. The halls varied in size from St John the Baptist, High Wycombe, founded *c.* 1180 for four inmates, to St Leonard's, York, refounded by King Stephen for 206 inmates. The hospital of St Cross at Winchester (*c.* 1150) was intended for the relief of thirteen poor men and the provision of daily doles to one hundred men of good conduct.

Tobit gives bread to the hungry and clothes to the naked, from Apocrypha initial, twelfth-century English Bible. (MS. Laud Misc. 752, 314r)

Leprosy was common in the twelfth century, particularly in towns. Disfigurement associated with the disease was seen by many as divine punishment for sin and carried the danger of moral contamination, and it was believed that the treatment of leprosy required seclusion from others. At Canterbury, Lanfranc built wooden houses 'in a more remote place to the north of the west gate of the city ... on the downward slope of a hill and assigned them for the use of lepers'.

Strict rules were laid down regarding the conduct and organisation of lepers, and committal to a 'lazar house' was a life sentence. After prayers a new leper was led to the house where he was to live 'as if he were dead'. By 1200 there were local laws forbidding lepers to enter towns. At Berwick-upon-Tweed:

> No leper shall come within the gates of the borough and if one gets in by chance, the serjeant shall put him out at once ... his clothes shall be taken off him and burnt and he shall be turned out naked.

It was believed that if a person led a good life salvation would follow, but a bad life would lead to eternal damnation. Souls, often judged by the archangel Michael, would be divided: the blessed to heaven, and the damned to hell. It was believed that sins could be wiped clean by penance or pilgrimage. When on his sickbed *c.* 1110, Nigel d'Aubigny wrote to the monks of Durham offering to return land that he had taken from them in order to avoid 'damnation of his soul' and 'everlasting hell'. Indeed, the urge to buy salvation for one's soul with last-minute grants to churches was so strong that twelfth-century English law did not recognise the validity of gifts of land made while the giver was on his deathbed.

When a Cluniac monk felt the moment of death approaching, he would summon his superior to hear his confession and receive extreme unction. At the moment of death, the man was laid on sackcloth and ashes in the shape of a cross, signifying penitence. The body was washed and then clothed in a hair shirt and hooded habit and placed on a bier. At the grave the body was censed and sprinkled with holy water, and then buried. The procession returned after the burial to the tolling of bells.

Next to the church, the churchyard or cemetery was the most holy place in a village, and horror of a non-church or non-cemetery burial was such that, apart from suicides and murderers, few were excluded. Most people were buried in a shroud and placed in a simple wooden coffin. Some burials were marked with a wooden cross, but this was not universal, and burial inside the church was reserved for senior churchmen and aristocratic patrons. When on his deathbed in 1181, Hugh de Mortimer was invested with

The Norman chapel of Stourbridge leper hospital, Cambridgeshire.

The Ladder of Salvation, wall painting, *c.* 1200, St Peter and St Paul's Church, Chaldon, Surrey. Images of the saved and the damned were common throughout medieval Europe.

the habit of an Augustinian canon by the abbot of Wigmore, the house which Hugh had endowed. On his death his 'body was carried to his abbey ... and interred honourably before the high altar', where his soul 'rests with God's chosen ones'.

The peasant was not free of the feudal system even in death, when a duty called the 'heriot' was levied on the family of the deceased by the lord. This was often in the form of his best animal. In addition the Church extracted a 'mortuary', which might also be one of the household's cows or pigs, while in towns the best robe would replace a beast. Most lay deaths would be marked by a vigil or wake and these were often accompanied by elaborate meals. It was the practice to summon rich and poor to pay their last respects. 'Wake ales' were brewed specially for the occasion, which often deteriorated through excessive drinking. Later Church councils denounced wakes as providing opportunities for fornication and theft.

A medieval cemetery at the deserted village of Wharram Percy, Yorkshire.

Grave goods from lay graves are virtually unknown from this period, although parish priests were buried with chalice and paten, and bishops, archbishops and royalty were buried in full ceremonial robes. One curious and poignant twelfth-century burial comes from the deserted village of Upton (Gloucestershire), where the bones of a baby were found under the floor of a peasant house. With it was an exotic shell and a spindle whorl, the latter being credited with supernatural properties.

PLACES TO VISIT

Battle Abbey, Battle, East Sussex HR2 9DN.

The Benedictine abbey at Battle was built by King William on the site of the Battle of Hastings, the high altar on the spot where King Harold was slain. There is a walk around the battlefield.

Boothby Pagnell, Grantham, Lincolnshire NG33 4DQ.

A rare example of a surviving stone manor house of about 1200, originally part of a larger house which lay within a defensive moat.

Bury St Edmunds Abbey, Bury St Edmunds, Suffolk IP33 1UN.

The tower gate is the most impressive survival from the great abbey, and is claimed to be the purest example of Norman architecture in England. *Moyse's Hall*, close by, is a Norman town house with a first-floor hall.

Castle Acre Priory, Castle Acre, Norfolk PE32 2AR.

Remains of twelfth-century Cluniac priory, incorporating fine blank arcading on west front of church. Nearby substantial earthworks of contemporary castle. Village laid out in an enclosure attached to castle.

Conisbrough Castle, Doncaster, West Riding of Yorkshire, DN12 3BU.

Late Norman cylindrical keep, built by Hamelin Plantagenet *c.* 1180.

Dover Castle, Kent CT16 1HU.

Henry II's great keep lies within a circuit of Roman and later defences. The Kings Hall, Guest Hall and Chamber house a remarkable collection of twelfth-century furnishings and artefacts.

Durham Cathedral, County Durham DH1 3EH.

The cathedral, built largely between 1093 and 1130, is England's premier Norman church. The incised drum pillars are particularly impressive. Close by is Durham Castle, the interior of whose chapel provides a remarkable example of early Norman work.

Hospital of St Cross, Winchester, Hampshire SO23 9SD.

St Cross is the oldest working hospital in England. This remarkable institution was founded by Bishop Henry de Blois, King Stephen's brother, in the mid-twelfth century. Only the church is a Norman building, but the hospital's layout is medieval.

Kilpeck Church, Kilpeck, Herefordshire HR2 9DN.

A fine example of a late Norman church with a remarkable carved south doorway and grotesque corbel table. There is a motte and bailey castle in the field to the west.

Kirkstall Abbey, Leeds, West Yorkshire LS5 3EH.

Remains of late-twelfth-century Cistercian Abbey, in places standing to its original height. Provides a unique impression of Norman monasticism.

Ludlow Castle, Ludlow, Shropshire SY8 1EJ.

One of the finest Welsh Border Norman castles, it was built by Roger de Lacy in the late eleventh century. It has a fine keep (originally a gatehouse) and a rare example of a circular chapel.

Museum of London, London Wall, London EC2Y 5HN.

The museum contains a large collection of early medieval artefacts, many of them domestic objects illustrating aspects of Norman England.

Museum of Reading, Reading, Berkshire RG1 1QH.

The museum houses a life-size Victorian replica of the Bayeux Tapestry.

Norwich Castle, Norwich, Norfolk NR13 JU.

One of the finest castle palaces in Europe, built between 1100 and 1120. Work on Norwich Cathedral, close by, started at the same time.

Oakham Castle, Oakham, Rutland LE15 6DX.

The best example of a surviving Norman baronial hall in England. Built between 1180 and 1190 by Walkelin de Ferrars. Contains some fine twelfth-century secular carving.

Old Sarum, Salisbury, Wiltshire SP1 3SD.

Site of the original Salisbury Cathedral, Norman town and bishop's castle contained within the reinforced defences of an Iron Age hill fort.

Pevensey Castle, Pevensey, East Sussex BN24 5LE.

Early Norman castle built within a Roman fort, formerly on the coast. William landed his army and camped here before the Battle of Hastings.

Restormel Castle, Lostwithiel, Cornwall PL22 0EE.

Good example of an eleventh-century motte and bailey castle with twelfth-century shell keep.

St Mary's Church, Kempley, Gloucestershire GL18 3JH.

Parish church containing a unique series of New Testament Norman wall paintings. Over the south doorway is a contemporary tree of life tympanum.

St Mary's Church, Melbourne, Derbyshire DE73 8GJ.

Built on the lines of a miniature cathedral, in the mid-twelfth century for the dispossessed Bishop of Carlisle, forced south by the Scots. Contains much impressive grotesque carving.

Southwell Minster, Southwell, Nottinghamshire NG25 0HD.

An impressive early-twelfth-century church with characteristic twin Norman west towers. Contains carvings marking the change from eleventh-century geometric motifs to twelfth-century narrative sculpture.

The Tower of London, London EC3N 4AB.

At the heart of the Tower of London is the formidable White Tower, the best-known Norman building in England, started *c.* 1080 by William the Conqueror and completed by his son William II. On the first floor is the Chapel of St John *c.* 1190, a remarkably well-preserved example of early Norman architecture.

INDEX

Page numbers in italic refer to illustrations